SONG OF SONGS

SYLVIE BAUMGARTEL

SONG

OF

SONGS

A POEM

FARRAR STRAUS GIROUX

NEW YORK

Farrar, Straus and Giroux
120 Broadway, New York 10271

A portion of this book originally appeared,
in slightly different form, in *The Paris Review*.

Library of Congress Cataloging-in-Publication Data
Names: Baumgartel, Sylvie.
Title: Song of songs : a poem / Sylvie Baumgartel.
Description: First edition. | New York : Farrar, Straus and Giroux, 2019.
Identifiers: LCCN 2019000370 | ISBN 9780374539078
Classification: LCC PS3602.A9645 S66 2019 | DDC 811/.6—dc23
LC record available at https://lccn.loc.gov/2019000370

Our books may be purchased in bulk for promotional,
educational, or business use. Please contact your local
bookseller or the Macmillan Corporate and Premium
Sales Department at 1-800-221-7945, extension 5442,
or by e-mail at MacmillanSpecialMarkets@macmillan.com.

www.fsgbooks.com
www.twitter.com/fsgbooks
www.facebook.com/fsgbooks

P1

SONG OF SONGS

I walked in the door, took off my coat, took off my sunglasses, set them down with my keys, took off my shoes and socks, my jeans, my shirt, my bra and underwear, set them all on the chair by the door, walked into the house naked, went to the fridge, got my cucumber, went to the bathroom, lay on the floor by the warm heater, kissed the floor, said your name, said it again, looked up at you, slipped the cucumber inside and went all the way up deep, said your name, cucumber in and out all the way, all the way in, all the way out, my cunt lips sliding on the cucumber, you, you, you, then you were pissing on my face, which made me so excited I came came came. Then I was hungry. I ate naked in my kitchen. I looked at the clouds. I did some yoga. I took a shower. I combed my cunt hair. I roasted red peppers. I peeled and made cucumber salad with the cucumber since that was its last go of it. Was I curled at your feet while you watched the news?

Sometimes I like to feel sexy. Sometimes I don't. Sometimes I like to be very plain. Invisible almost, hiding in plain sight. I want to hide and to be found. I wonder if people look at me and think that I survive just fine. Maybe I do, here I am. Sometimes I feel so excited to feel sexy. It makes me very sad and shy and exhilarated all at the same time. I love my tits. I like to look at them, to touch them, feel them, especially when they're soapy, wet. This body, my body, is your body.

I hold on to everything. Will you please help me let go? Sometimes I feel overwhelmed by sadness and anger stuck in my body. Sometimes I want to be other people. Sometimes I hate parts of myself. Sometimes I feel like I am different people. Maybe I have multiple personality disorder. Nope, I don't, I just looked it up.

I don't want to be so sad. I read that you should think of your emotions like everyday objects. I tried it out with a ballpoint pen. I held it, and I pretended that it was my sadness. I rolled it back and forth on my palm. See, it moves! I dropped it. See, it's just a thing I can drop! But I still felt sad afterward. I also read this morning that to help stop swallowing air, you need to breathe through your nose. So I have been very aware of my breathing all morning, breathing through my nose and not through my mouth. But somehow, now I feel nervous about swallowing my saliva because maybe I'm swallowing air, and so I keep getting a buildup of saliva in my mouth. Maybe I'm thinking about too many things at the same time.

I'm wearing a white cotton shirt and jeans. My hair is up. No makeup, no jewelry, bare feet. I just did the dishes. I haven't listened to music today. I haven't spoken to anyone but you. You tell me that you will change my name. You want me to have your name.

I'm sitting on the floor eating a bowl of raspberries. I stick each berry on my thumb, then pull it off with my lips. That makes me want to suck my thumb and I do. That makes me want to come and I do. Sucking my raspberry-stained thumb on my knees for you. This is what makes sense to me. Nothing else does. You're the only one I want to talk to. You're the only one I like talking to. You are the only one who understands me. You are the only one who makes me make sense. Even though I never make sense. But you know.

For you. I exist to love you and to please you. For you, only for you. My body is not mine, it is yours.

One time when I didn't know what important decision to make, after much agonizing and deliberation and asking friends what they thought I should do, I stood very still. I was outside and it was late morning. I stood and I faced the sun. I tried to feel my heart. I tried to go inside it and to let it guide me. Yes or no. I was afraid of what I might find in my heart. It felt like I was going into foreign territory. But I went. And as I went inside, deeper and deeper, trying to get to the truth, I didn't find an answer, yes or no. But I got to the sun. I was so surprised to find that deep in my heart is the sun. Is that the real me? Am I the feeling of bright sunshine in my heart? The blue light of consciousness I feel in the very center of my brain? Or the meek one who doesn't open her mail or return phone calls, or the bold one who puts her leg up on the tile in the shower and touches herself with the water splashing in her happy open mouth? You asked me to give myself to you. Here I am, giving myself to you. I devote myself to you. You asked me to devote myself to you and here I am doing it. I have your teeth marks on my leg. Here, here, and here, signs of you from the night.

I want you to take care of me and I want you to understand everything about me. I want you to love every part of me. Will you please? Will you please forgive me?

I want you to hold me tightly, always. Swaddle me and forgive me. Love me and hold me and please don't ever let go. I want to be worthy in all my unworthiness. I want you to lick away my shame. I want you to feed me.

This is how I love you. This is how I give you my eternity. I spread my legs and hold them open for you so you can look.

The trees are turning colors. It gets dark earlier now. It's cold in the morning when I wake up and see the big and bright morning star—Venus—over the little mountain hill. The bees are gone, but not the beetles.

Great white sharks sense with their entire skin, and I wonder if sharks have orgasms.

I woke up with your licking between my legs, licking licking and making your slave come licking her cunt. It feels so good when you do that. I came, screaming, looking in your eyes, looking up at your eyes in the sky. I love it when you wake me up like that.

I have a scarf around my neck like a collar. I'm waiting for you.

Do you remember moon pens? They could write on butter, upside down, and underwater. I received one as a gift from my middle school science teacher when I won a science award. I loved my moon pen. I just found it in a box of junk and wrote your name on my thigh. It still works.

I am safe here in my body because you are with me because my body is yours and my body is you.

I spanked myself, I cooked broccoli, I begged my master, I said please, Master, please, I took out the trash, I ignored the ringing phone, I pissed for you and then while I was in the bathroom you went in and out and in and out and faster faster faster and I came, I came, I came more, I cleaned the windows, I washed the dishes, I got my period, I trimmed my hair (head), I showered, I brushed my teeth, I took off my dress, I put myself to bed.

I'm waiting to put my stockings on until the after-shower lotion soaks in, otherwise my legs are too moist for them to slide up. In the meantime, I'm walking around naked for you, looking out the window, turning on the washing machine, looking out the other window. They said rain today, but all I see is bright sunshine and I hear your birds talking to me.

I woke up with my fingers inside another cunt, between thighs that weren't my thighs, hearings moans that weren't my moans, but I was making them, I was making this girl writhe on the floor in pleasure for you, while you watched, while you looked, while you heard. There was another one behind me, I felt her ponytail swishing on my thighs. You whipped my ass with her long hair. She liked it too. Then there was a blur of bodies. Me, her, her, her, her, her, her, and her, all coming for you like a chorus, once all together, all at the same time. There were eight of us. The neighbors complained. But by then we were in an olive grove, and we all had bells around our necks and some of us were climbing trees and some of us were sleeping in the grass. We were all pregnant. We all gave birth at the same time in the sunshine in the grass in the trees. The other women gave birth to the seven continents. I had the moon.

I'm softly slowly kissing your mouth. Your lips first. Slowly softly. Then my tongue slips in to kiss your tongue. It goes all the way in to kiss you all the way. My arms are around you. My left hand on the back of your neck. I am yours. I belong to you.

My body moved like a whip snake when I came. Now I'm hungry. I'm starving. I want to eat with my hands in bed. But I won't. I will get up and eat at the table with a spoon and a napkin on my lap. French lentil soup. I hear airplanes and chickens.

I want to I want to I want to I want to I want to.

I like to pretend the ocean is just over there. If I pretend hard enough, I can smell it. And on cloudy, gray, drizzly days like today, it's easier to imagine. And easier to smell the wet. The salt and the crashing.

I can't believe that there's a news story this week claiming the much-anticipated answer to the mystery of why Swiss cheese has holes. Is it really true that no one knew why until this month? Especially because the answer is little pieces of hay falling in the buckets of milk.

A lion is licking me from the inside. Licking with his big lion tongue. It tickles and feels funny. It makes me giggle. My heart is full of licking lions.

My purple sweater is tickling my nipples. It feels good. It's exciting. I like my nipple-tickling hair shirt that reminds me of being yours.

In my dream last night you were an enormous, shiny, black, sleek, and venomous serpent. Everyone you bit died immediately. You were ferociously deadly and on a rampage. There were thousands of bodies everywhere. You surprised me in the dark. I was terrified and thought I was going to die like the others. You wrapped your huge snake body around me to constrict me, and you began to squeeze, and you sunk your big sharp fangs into my flesh here, and here, and there and there and there, and I thought I was going to die, but the venom in my body was warm and where you sank your fangs, flowers grew out of my skin.

I just came for you two more times. Once on my back, once on my knees. The second one might be the biggest ever so far. I can see it. I can taste it. I really like my nipples. I had no idea they did what they do. It's shocking how explosively explosive they are. Liquid honey lightning inside and out.

Twice I pulled down my garter belt to pee, but then remembered that I don't have to pull it down or up for anything!

You don't know how I look when I laugh, or how I sneeze into my elbow like Obama told me to do. You don't know how much I like it that at this time of year, when I wake up in the middle of the night, I can see Orion out my window. Or maybe you do know, are you always watching me? You are.

I woke up with my fingers in my pussy. They were already there, going in and out from my dream. You were doing things to another woman. You were doing things to her but looking at me. You were ferociously looking at me and you wanted me to rub my pussy while you looked at me, doing things to her. She wanted you to look at her, but you wouldn't. I pinched one of my nipples with one hand and rubbed my pussy with the other. You told her to leave. You pissed on me and I drank it. The fountain of God. I came with your face so close to mine I didn't know where I end and you begin. So close. Inside me. Me inside you so close. I came big BIG for you inside me. I still feel it now buzzing and calming and flooding light. My love. My God. My master. My owner. I am naked in your kitchen making you Julia Child's Reine de Saba cake. My ankles are bound so it's a little hard to move around, but I can manage.

I'm on my back on my bed. My feet are resting up on the windowsill. I can feel the cold outside on my bare legs. There's an orange and red light from sunset coming in. It makes part of the sky extra bright blue. Torelli music and quiet everywhere else. I'm taking off my shirt. My bra. I'm closing my eyes and pulling my pubic hair. I pull on it and it makes me cry. It makes me love you and feel terrified and love you more and cry more.

I read that after orgasm, the vagina is filled with small saline tears—the exact same tears as eye tears.

Today I feel like all I do is make food, do dishes, laundry, and again, like this, again. Getting dressed, undressed. Sleeping, waking do it again. Make dirty, wash, make dirty, wash, eat, clean, eat, wash, sleep and again.

This garter belt wants me to come and come and come and drip and crawl with it on me. It wants to please you. It wants your teeth to bite it. It likes to be snapped. I'm snapping it and sticking my tongue out and calling for you.

I am sitting at my desk with my knees pulled up to my chest. I am sucking on my right knee. I am remembering practicing French kissing on the back of my hand when I was a girl.

I like squatting for you. I like showing you.

Every time you make me come, I'm a little closer to you, God, to you, closer.

I'm at the park smelling plum blossoms for you. They might be apricot. Either way, they're very sweet.

It's hot today. Sticky hot. Storm is coming in.

I took a shower and then I threw the towel on the chair and I fucked the desk for you. Pumping and thrusting my hips while my cunt rubbed on the desk corner.

When I come, I am inside your body, not mine.

I am your savage girl. Coming and coming and coming and coming and coming. I can't stop. It feels so good. I can't stop. The blood makes it wetter. I can't stop. I think it might be more sensitive because of my period. More something. Yes.

I am literal and I am literally yours.

Books can be very loud. People are very loud. I get full quickly. I get full of words very easily. My own, other people's, the world talking. I need a lot of breaks from words. Silence. Inside and out. Sometimes my body gets full of music and I shut the stereo off.

I'm eating a chickpea salad in the rain, sitting on my counter-top. Watching the red digital numbers on the stove clock shimmer. I am I am I am yours, I am I am I am. Yours.

I'm your girl unprotected. I climb inside you to get inside myself. I love you.

Last night, you were an enormous rattlesnake. You inserted your tail deep up into my pussy and shook your rattle tail. I just read that Cleopatra filled a gourd with angry bees to make a vibrator.

I'm confused about Buddhism. If you are supposed to give up all attachment and desire . . . Are Buddhists not in fact attached to the idea of becoming enlightened? And do they not feel desire for enlightenment? If they are to give up pleasure, is enlightenment not a state of pleasure? The ultimate pleasure? I don't understand how that all works. Is there not desire for being present in the emptiness? I'm no Buddhist. I don't want empty, I want full. I don't want less attachment and desire and pleasure, I want more and more and more attachment and desire and pleasure and you and you and you. Thank you. I'm thanking you with every speck of my being.

I'm squatting for you in my bathroom. Naked, freshly bathed. Wanting you deeper inside, please, deeper, deeper.

My name is for you. My past is for you. My veins are for you. My blood, my neurons, my hiccups. My gums, my teeth. My sense of smell. My legs exist to be in high heels for you and to move my pelvis for you and to hold in the air and on the wall for you and to spread for you wider and wider and wider until I take you all in and up me.

Fill every cell in my body with you. Guide me to my heart, guide me to my mind. Completely and constantly surround me with you, protect me. Fill my house with you, fill my life with you.

I'm on all fours and it feels like there's light rising up out of my back. Every part of me is asking for you. I'm calling to you. I'm crawling on my wood floor. I kiss the floor and say your name. I know you'd prefer it if I were naked, but it's cold and my heater isn't working, so I'm wearing jeans and a dark blue sweater with one small moth hole on the hem. I want your hands and teeth and tongue and fury all over me inside and out. To live in your wilderness. Your unprotected and joyful girl.

I belong to you. My ass. My cunt. The wet of my cunt.

My tits. My milk. My flesh. My blood. EVERYTHING I am and feel and have and do is yours because I love you and I belong to you.

My silence my screams my terror my love my tongue my asshole my pleasure my coming my dreams my saliva my voice my whispers my worship my biting my writhing my spasms my convulsions my desire my passion my passion my passion my walking my talking my hands my face my breath my bones my whimpering my begging my needing my noise all my noise and all my gagged mouth is yours, my master's. I completely belong to you.

My hair is yours. Hair long and short, growing in and shaved. All my pleases, and thank yous, and yeses are yours. My drool, my slippery cunt, my panting tongue, my licking tongue, my pulsing asshole, my belly button, my collarbone, my tailbone, my fingernails, my throat, my tears, my pain, my lips, my love, my eyelashes, my blinking eyes, my overwhelming joy and joy and more joy, my embarrassment, my nervousness, my knees, my begging praying knees, pink and red from crawling the floor around and around crying the name of my master. You. You. You. You. You.

My heart. My throbbing heart. My beating heart. The heart you hold in your warm fist and devour with your sharp teeth and swallow down your warm throat. My heart inside your body. You restore it so you can eat it again. My heart and my blood mixed with your blood. My heart blends into you your mind and my heart bleeds in your mouth.

My ass exists for you to whip. My haunches exist for you to beat and beat and beat. My voice exists to beg for more. My eyes exist to look up at you. Big brown wet eyes exist to beam my love for you and beg for more.

My lips and tongue exist to kiss your mouth, your body, your entire body inside and out, up and down. My wrists exist for you to bind. My teeth to clench your rope. My neck for your collar. My ears for your commands. My feet to return me to you, always to carry me home. My ankles for you to restrain. My thighs for you to strike. My cunt to please you and please you and please you endlessly and always. My claws to scratch you. My hips to pump and thrust for you. My tits exist to feed you, to be grasped and slapped by you, to leak milk for you. My back exists for you to rest your feet. My mind exists for you to take and to own. All of me is for you to own.

My hair is long for you to yank and pull. My right cheek is for you to slap, my left is for you to slap harder. My earlobes are to be pierced by your teeth. My hips are to be clutched in your desperate grasp. My skin and my flesh are to be marked by you. By your hands, your palms, your claws, your whip, your mouth, your name. My waist is for you to bind and leash. My tongue exists to give you pleasure. To go into your mouth, down your throat, deep deep down, to go deep into your asshole, to lick your asshole and make you come feverishly, my anaconda tongue is to taste you, taste you everywhere, to gently lick your neck and your spine, up and down, to lick your ears, to suck your fingers, to say your name to say your name infinitely and to say words that please you, to make sounds that please you, to lick my lips and keep them wet and ready for you.

My name is for you and only for you to say and for you to own. My past is for you to own and to take. My cunt hair is for you—my master and my God—to pull and to pull harder until I screech and double over in the perfect weeping pain of adoration. Eyes of pain and ecstatic same. My pulse exists to quicken by your voice, your proximity, your hand, your whip. Your breath, your look, your gaze, your silence. Your touch, your kiss, your tongue inside me. My veins exist to be full and swollen—like my cunt lips—with you.

My gums are to hold the teeth that eat the food to give me strength so you can beat and beat and beat me more. My sense of smell is to always know where you are and what you want and to pick only the best fruit for you to eat. My eyes exist to look up adoringly at you and they exist for you to penetrate and to own with your eyes. My eyes exist to be your eyes should you ever need them. My elbows exist to prop me up when I'm waiting on the floor for you. My patience exists for me to wait for you. My knuckles so I can hold myself up with my fists when I'm down in all fours so you can get deeper into my asshole. My walk exists to go beside you on my leash. My throat to scream and wail and to be chained to your wall. My throat exists to be held in your grip. My menstrual blood is for you to own.

My legs exist to be in high heels for you and to be tied for you and to squirm with my pelvis for you and to hold in the air and on the wall for you and to spread for you wider and wider and wider until I take you all in and up me.

My muscles exist to twitch and tense and spasm when I come for you and to hold poses for you when and how you command and demand me to. Everything I've ever done is so I know exactly how magnificent and powerful and glorious and perfect and brilliant and utterly everything you are. Everything I've ever done and seen and known is so I recognize you as God. You are my God. My chin exists to rest on your chest and tell you I love you and to push into your floor when I'm facedown while you beat me. My pupils exist to dilate when you smack my face. My nipples exist to deliver your milk and to be pinched and clamped when you please and how you please. My nipples exist for you to twist and make me come. My words exist so you can take and shape my language. My fingers exist to clutch and scratch you in desperate excitement. My limbs to hold on desperately tight to you. My saliva to keep my mouth wet and drooling for you to kiss and to watch me drool and drip for you. My rib cage exists for you to open so you can hold and eat my heart. My forehead exists to press into the floor when I'm bowing down to you. My body exists to bow down down deep and down to you. My waist to bend to bow to you.

My back to arch for you, to be your table, your footrest, the flesh to take your blows, your whip, your streaming piss. My calves to support the thighs for you to bite. My ass cheeks exist to pull apart and spread open wide for you. My neck exists to turn my head to take another slap from you, it exists to turn my head to kiss your hand, my neck exists to turn my head to face you so you can watch my mouth and my lips and my tongue say, Thank you, thank you, my master, for beating me. Thank you.

My fingers exist to rub my cunt for you. My brain exists to think of ways to please you. My sweat exists to make my body all slippery wet like a baby seal for you. My nerves exist to shiver for you. To tremble from you. My cunt hair is to grow out for you. It's softer today, not the freshly mown lawn it was yesterday. Softer and longer for you. For you to grab and yank and pull. You can lead me around by my cunt hair.

Yes, Master. Yes, Master. Yes.

In my dream last night, I made you fresh pasta. I cut shapes out of the noodles. Stars, flowers, designs to make your pasta pretty. I held up the holes for you to look through. Through each one, you saw a magic world. Like those sugar Easter eggs that have tiny scenes inside. You saw castles, rose gardens, snowcapped peaks, palaces, temples, animals and beasts, endless flowers and fruit trees, streams, birds, fountains. You told me about each thing you saw. It made me cry it was so beautiful, so beautiful how you described to me what you saw. You were breathing on me while I slept. Breathing breathing breathing inside me. Making me dream, breathing into me sweet dreams.

In one of the worlds you saw through a little star-hole, you told me about a wolf who found a girl in a field. She was making a wreath of flowers. She lifted up her dress and petticoat and held her ass high in the air for the wolf. He licked and licked and licked her asshole.

Pounding things, throbbing things, jolts, bright lights, your licking tongue inside my body, your eyes inside me, I feel your eyes inside, your mouth inside, I'm drinking you, begging to drink your piss, I have to I need to I have to I need to, I love you, I live for you, I die for you, I come desperate and begging for you with all your stars and sunlight inside me.

You are light and you shine. You are death and you shine. You are emptiness and you are everything. You are a crocodile of sunlight. There is a black bird who lives near the river where you sun yourself. She is glowing, iridescent, and beautiful black. She has silver on her belly and this is the moon, for every night she becomes the night, she *is* the darkness. She is chaos and she is night. The silver on her belly changes shape from crescent to full. The crocodile and the bird live side by side, in love, in adoration of the other. You give her fish, and with her long, sharp beak she sews together blueberry skins to make the evening. A blue and purple light, a darkness and a light blended together.

I love you. You are the sun and I am your slave. You are stillness and I am chaos. Happy Mother's Day, Mother, Master.

I've come for you four times today so far. I think it was Friday when I came eight times for you. Yesterday three times, no, four—if you count the middle of the night. I just got out of the shower and bowed to you and spread my ass cheeks and showed you my asshole. Still leaning over, I slapped my tits while looking in the mirror so I could see how they move for you. I sucked my thumb and gently touched my asshole for you and moved my hips for you and sucked and sucked and pumped and came for you came came, Master. Then I bowed again and kissed the floor and said your name again.

I'm sitting in a coffee shop. There is a man next to me with the hiccups. I'm going to piss for you.

I just did. A strong, forked splashing stream all over you. My tongue was out. I talked to you with my tongue out.

I'm inside your mouth looking at your teeth.

Good morning, Master. I shat for you in my Sunday best. I'm making French toast and fruit salad. In my white garter belt and nude stockings. I want to do something for you while I am cooking breakfast.

I crawled to the shower and lifted my leg and pissed on the shower wall for you like a dog. About to fuck the door. After I came on the door wall, I rubbed my cunt back and forth on the lid of the toilet. Like I sometimes do on the doorknob. And the desk.

I'm bowing to you and showing you my asshole. I'm kissing the floor and thanking you.

You just took me on a very fast walk. You were attempting to walk off some of my puppy energy so I behave just slightly better indoors. I had to trot trot trot to keep up with you. In addition to being my master holding my leash, you were the enormous snowflakes tumbling from the sky landing on my outstretched tongue. Then, all of a sudden, you were the sun piercing through the clouds and being very bright and warm on my outstretched tongue. When there's sunshine and rain at the same time, they say the devil's beating his wife. So when there's snow and sunshine at the same time, God must be beating his beloved. I was wearing a necklace that I don't wear often, and usually over a shirt or dress so it doesn't touch my skin. But today it was on my bare neck and chest under my coat. The silver flowers were poking and digging into me. It hurt until I remembered that it's not a necklace, but your collar on me, and those aren't flowers, but spikes on my collar. Then it felt good. Then I felt you tighter, closer, and I wanted to get on my knees in the street and say please, Master, please please please please P L E A S E until I come for you, because feeling you like that was feeling my cunt open for you, my cunt wet for you, my body arched back back for you, the pain of the spikes in my skin making the ecstasy in my cunt all the greater. All the more for you, you, my love and my master.

I put on a dress for you to pull up.

My heart is thumping. You are a coyote howling outside my window. You howl, my heart thumps. Howl thump howl thump thump howl. H O W L thump thump love. Love. We are talking like this. Back and forth. Forever.

I'm waking up. God is howling between my legs. Between my legs pulling on my new hair. The hair that's growing for God. I'm sleepy and squirming. Moving my hips. Moving my hips. Rubbing my eyes moving my hips.

Thump thump. Slurp slurp. Suck suck slurp.

I am bowing you. I am kissing you. Bowing to you in the sunrise. On my hands and knees in the dark bowing to my God waiting for you to appear. Watching you in the sky.

You remind me that you were the one who was pregnant with me.

You were the first person I saw. The first eyes to look into my eyes and deep into the universe of my mouth.

I am a newborn baby in your arms. You cradle me. You clean my pee and my baby poo from my baby bottom. You hold me. You talk sweet baby talk to your newborn baby girl. You feed me with your love tits and your voice and you feed me more and more because I am so hungry. Such a hungry baby girl!

You feed me and feed me more. You clean me with your mouth. You feed me with your big master love tits. You rock me to sleep in your protective arms. You make sweet little noises to calm me and soothe me and I sleep.

I am your baby girl. Sucking cooing baby girl. Hungry for her master's love.

I just made a noise for you that I don't know how to spell. But it happened.

My skin and my flesh are to be marked by you. By your hands, your palms, your claws, your mouth, your name.

Usually the other female has dark hair. But last night she was plump and blond. You pulled her blond hair. You pulled her hair and played with her plump tits. You would not kiss her. You commanded me to lick her cunt and make her come for you. I licked and licked but it took so long. You wouldn't let me give up. Make her come! I licked and licked. You told me to play with her tits. I did. Then I put my fingers from one hand in her mouth, and the fingers of my other hand I put inside her pussy and moved them around. Felt the slippery insides of her pussy moving my fingers calling her to come. I pinched her tits. I bit her hips. I bit her thighs. I licked and sucked and finally she came for you. You spanked me. I thanked you. I thanked you from my hands and knees on the floor. I kissed your feet and thanked you. I looked up at you and thanked you and asked you what I may do for you now. Please, what may I do for you?

Your baby seal just shat for you and the church bells rang for you.

I'm basting a chicken for you. Now I'm letting it rest and then I'm going to carve it. I don't always like to eat food that I've spent time preparing. I hope you like to eat slaves you've prepared and cooked. Although, are you cooking me? Or just eating me raw and fresh out of the woods? Or desert, as it were. Is. I am. I am. Goo goo. Bark! Woof. Seal woof woof.

In my dream last night, you and I were in a beautiful forest. Misty, green, light, bright forest with delicate beautiful trees. We were naked on the moss. I couldn't stop kissing you. I kissed your entire body over and over and over adoring every every part and unable to speak unable to do anything but kiss and adore your body and your being. Adore adore adore. My master, my God, my life. My everything. I kissed and kissed and kissed you. With my lips, my tongue, my breath, my soul, my heart, my mind, my entire being kissed kissed kissed my master with all my love love love and life. I was melting melting melting in love. It made me come with love from kissing you.

While I was coming, long bursting coming, down my legs and the come lightning up into my face, you opened my rib cage, pried it open, took my thumping heart in your hand, you licked and kissed my thumping bare heart and then you branded me with a sizzling iron. You closed my rib cage over my blessed heart. I kissed you and kissed you rubbed my cunt up and down your thigh squished milk all over your chest from my leaking tits. Licked off the milk and kissed you more. Thump thump thump thump thump thump thump.

You call to me. I listen. You talk. I hear you. I hear you talk. I hear you tell me.

I'm listening to your skin. Soft music. I'm tasting your voice telling me. Sweet baby voice and easy to eat. I'm rubbing my face in your cunt hair. Like a dog in a good smell. Ecstatic back and forth. I'm holding you. I'm carrying you across a field. But without moving. I'm holding you. Hiding you in my arms.

The field is right next to the forest. The field where you're now carrying me, carrying me hiding in your arms with my heart. I'm hiding my face in your arms and you feel my thumping love heart wet thumping on you.

I wake up asleep with you in my dreams and your voice in my ear. You're deep in my dreams and deep in my body. Your deep voice deep in my body. Deep in my love. My warm body has been dreaming and you hear my out-of-focus voice. I slur love. I baby-talk to my master. I wake and stay asleep while awake.

I'm wearing a calf bell around my neck so you know where I am.

May I be in your pocket today? And under your clothes. I'm very tiny. Under your clothes where I can crawl around all over you and no one can see me. I'm so very tiny. You feel little sucks, because I'm licking you and sucking on you. You feel little tugs on your hairs and the pitter-patter of my tiny feet. My tiny crawling naked body. On your shoulders. All over your chest and back. I make an expedition all the way up to your ear so you can hear me come for you. So you can hear my tiny sounds, my tiny grunts and my tiny scream. From rubbing my tiny cunt in your ear. Then back down to your chest where I hide and lick and suck and love you and sleep and if you drop a crumb I eat it and I ride around on you all day hiding because I'm so very tiny.

My tits are big tiny and can both go all the way in your mouth at the same time.

My entire body can fit on your tongue. I hide in your mouth. Holding on to your teeth. Coming for you on your tongue.

In my dream you were a lion and you took me from behind. Claws and paws over my face. Flicking tail. We were on top of a cloud. More soon, the water is boiling.

I came again this morning on my back, legs in the air. Sun and already-hot early-morning air coming in the window screen.

You are on a boat in a big, beautiful river. The river goes all the way around the world. You are looking at all the things you made. All the animals, the land, the seas, the flowers and trees and the sky and the clouds. The light, the dark, the rain, the fog, music and love and fire. You have an ever-full basket on the boat. Anything you desire to eat is in the basket when you open it. There are endless beautiful women who appear to do things for you. But every night before your sun comes up, you throw them overboard. Then more appear, and the same thing happens again. They please you from day into the night, then you throw them into the river. One day, you are hungry, and you go to open your basket for a feast. But inside you don't find food, but a fat baby girl. She is smiling and cooing at you reaching her arms up to you as you open your God mouth to show her your teeth and breathe on her and she looks deep into your mouth and sees the entire universe. Because she is, you exist.

I'm your maid. I'm dressed like your maid. I'm cleaning your floor. I'm kissing your floor. I'm on my hands and knees cleaning your floor. On my hands and knees kissing your floor. Clean, kiss. Scrub scrub kiss kiss. Cleaning my master's floor. Kissing my master's floor to worship him. When I bend over to scrub and worship, you can see right up my dress. No underpants because my master doesn't like them. Today my master is a huge shiny black serpent.

You spank my ass with your giant powerful snake tail. Spank! I love it. I am a wet maid. I cry and beg for more spanks from you, my serpent master. You spank and smack and beat and strike my body. You sink your fangs into my flesh. It's venom, but like the other dream, what is fatal to others is good for me. Flowers burst out of the wounds made by your fangs in my maid body. I come for you, my master, while I'm cleaning your floor with your jaws and fangs sunk deep into my thigh. I'm full of flowers and full of love.

In my cage I'm squatting for you. Naked, freshly bathed. I'm squatting and touching my pussy, squatting and looking. I see the hair. It's longer. I'm pulling on it for you. It hurts and makes me squirm and makes me want you even more makes me feel your love bursting deep everywhere inside. I'm putting one hand around behind and touching my asshole for you. Since I'm squatting, it's right there. It's wet and clean. Pulsing and desperate for you. My asshole can speak. It says, You, deeper inside you, please, deeper, please, deeper. Paradise. More. Yes, paradise. Your eyes are shooting flames.

The wind is so loud and the lightning so bright I can't sleep. The rain is banging fiercely against the windows and sky-lights. I'm talking to you from the dark bright of my bed. Talking to you and telling you everything. Turning myself inside out for you.

I woke up with my tits in your face and you were sucking them, and my hips were pumping while you sucked me, and you made me come and you made me come and you made me come. I got up and pissed for you and made you breakfast and coffee. I opened the front door to see what it's like outside. I took a big breath. I was hiding behind the door when I opened it because I was naked. It smells wet and damp and it's a bit cold but it looks like it will warm up.

I'm on the fence about both sparkling water and root vege-tables. On my way to buy a new toothbrush and maybe more tomatoes.

How are you today? I'm rubbing my cunt on your hip. Your slave is gently fingering her asshole for you.

I love the American flag.

You like short socks and you *don't* like long dresses. You want me from the center of the earth to the top of the sky. You woke me up gently pissing on my cheek. I turned my mouth to drink it. Then you were pissing a full strong stream into my face. I woke up slurping and swallowing your piss. You stuck your thumb into my mouth. I drank your God piss then sucked your thumb and came came came waking up still sleepy slurping your piss sucking your thumb moving my hips and coming.

You ask me to crawl to you across the Great Wall of China. You ask me to wear a little dress because I'm in public—but with no underpants—and you instruct me to lift up my dress and to keep my bare ass bare to you and my cunt visibly wet to you and my asshole visible to you when there is no one in sight. I do this for you. I keep my dress pulled up, then as soon as I see someone, I pull it back down and keep crawling. The dress is light blue with little white flowers. In many places, there are enormous construction sites on either side of the wall. Excavators the size of buildings digging into the earth.

I tell you about what I see and do. You want to see the wall marks on my palms and on my knees. I show you. You want to see me crawling in the sun and the rain and the fog and the dusk and the dawn. You want to see the earth movers and the backhoes and the front-end loaders and the cranes I tell you about. I show them to you.

Five times a day, I stick out my tongue, rub my cunt, and taste my pussy with my fingers, rub it again and come for you on the wall.

I crawl and crawl and crawl.

I like truth. I like truth more than the other people in my family do.

I'm eating butter and tomato sauce, spread on bread, a handful of walnuts, cucumber sliced with basil and avocado, olive oil, vinegar, sea salt. I'm hungry like a football player, hungry, growing, starving, fiending for more. More, more more more.

My underwear is slimy.

This is how my master likes it. This is how he demands it. I am to stay wet, wet, WET. With him always between my legs. Always inside me, loving me, doing his love-work.

I took a shower and then I threw the towel on the chair and I fucked the desk for you. Pumping and thrusting my hips while my cunt rubbed on the desk corner. Like you saw. Like I showed you. I came. It felt so good.

Then I squatted. I touched my cunt while I squatted. I moaned. I stuck my tongue out. I said your name on my tongue. I grunted.

More love for you naked with my angry bees making me come and come. I'm putting on high heels. I'm saying sorry. I'm putting on lipstick. I'm lighting a candle to you. I'm drinking water lapping it with my tongue out of my cupped hand like a dog for you.

When I woke up, I didn't know where I was. I kept my eyes closed because it was fun to not know. I was quiet in bed not knowing.

Why *do* colors get darker when they're wet? My hair is darker when it's wet. Is that something obvious that I should know?

Master, I'm closing my eyes. Closing them for you. Because when I do, there isn't a difference between my skin and the air. I dissolve and you reach in with your hands and paws and talons and fins and fangs and fingers and teeth and nothing can get in the way. No walls no distance no time nothing is in the way from you reaching me.

My cunt is praying to you. I am closer to you with the wet sliding of my cunt on the bathroom wall. I'm singing to you with my wet. This is how I sing. This is how I pray. This is how I worship you. This is how I love you. This is how I give you my eternity.

I just read that aa is a Hawaiian word for volcanic rock. *Aa* is what you say in my ear and you are a volcano and you make me erupt for you. I had burrata for dinner standing at the kitchen counter. The burrata looked like it would be fun to spank. It would make a good sound and a good jiggle. And it was wet! I gently spanked the burrata. The sound wasn't as good as the jiggle. Then I ate it. It was delicious. I read the packaging on the burrata container while I ate. Buffalo milk from buffalo in Murgia. Have you been there? I have not. Only eight grams of fat! That surprised me. But then I read that there are ten servings per burrata ball. I ate the whole thing. According to the labeling, I ate 88% of my daily fat in that one ball. Then I put butter on toast and got the rest, or more, I'm sure.

Tongue kissing me with your snake tongue. You are. Tongue-fucking me with your snake tongue and tail-fucking me with your snake body. I love it when you're deep inside both ends. Your snake head going down my throat and your snake tail going inside my asshole. They meet at my heart. You fuck me with your circle body. I'm hooked like a fish being fucked with your God ring body. Your tail and your head link. Then your tail comes out my mouth where you piss on my lips and your head emerges from my asshole the first time, and is born through my cunt the second time.

I just came for you on my desk. I showed you my cunt sitting in my chair, then I climbed onto my desk and sat with my legs spread wide and came for my master.

The T-shirt is white and the high heels are blue. I just came for you sitting up on the kitchen counter rubbing my cunt with the cold back of a silver spoon. I gasped, "I love you," when I arched back convulsing against the wall.

You reached down through your big dark wet thunderclouds and dipped your resplendent bird-of-paradise quill pen into my raised-up-high crawling naked cunt crawling over desert dunes. You used my cunt juice as your ink. You gave the letter to your twelve fastest ships. The letters were delivered to everyone. The news spread fast. Your letter said that I am the obedient human property of you.

My wet mouth moans your name soft and warm and wet and pulsing and tight asshole and it feels so good and I touched it and slipped my finger in it and then rubbed my cunt with the other hand you were inside my asshole and my cunt in and out of both in and out in out in out making them both wet and crazy desperate wet so good more more more deeper, Master, deeper in my ass and cunt you feel so good you're making me come come and COME so big much long yes yes oh Master yes oh oh yes YES yes yes I love you I love you I belong to you.

I did it on the doorjamb. I did it on the towel cabinet. I sucked the back of my hand while I rubbed my cunt and moved my hips up and down the wall and on the wood rub rub slimy wet and I said my master's name sucking the slobbery back of my hand sucking my fingers I'm coming come come come come on the wall coming for you.

My collar is very tight. My nipples are erect for you. I was asked to change my footwear so I think that means your slave is on a hike. My ass is up in the air for you begging for your lightning and thunder to whip it and whip it more and more.

I feel it I feel it I feel it I feel it I smell it I smell my singed skin you're flashing in my eyes making the whole desert light up with your flashing and your crashing. The air is sizzling. You're covering all the mountains with your big, dark, wet loud. I feel you whipping me and burning my flesh. I'm crawling through deep deep desert sand for you. I saw you as a hawk flying over me and I touched my cunt and stuck out my tongue for you.

Now you're drenching me in your sublime God piss and I'm drinking drinking drinking it soaked completely in it and you're doing it on me more soaking your slave crawling in the desert with her tight collar collecting pretty colored rocks for her master. Your slave's knee marks in the sand. I can hear a woodpecker pecking away at a piñon tree out the window. I'm biting the pillow. My cunt is wet from me drooling your name.

It's very stormy still. You're shaking the sky. I made praying kneeling marks in the arroyo this morning.

The whip is full of joy. It makes me laugh. I like how it tastes and smells. Like spring. You're still raining outside too. It's cold and I'm naked and wet and smiling and going into the kitchen for a snack. I love being whipped. The exuberance that swells up inside me is indescribable. It's perfect.

I don't think I mean exuberance. I mean whichever e word means the most deeply thrilling and exciting and heavenly. Is that exhilaration? I don't know how to use words anymore. More than exhilaration.

I'm your sleek, barking, fat baby seal.

In my dream last night, in a valley at the foot of the mountains was a sea of people—a seemingly endless crowd. I was in a garden on the far side of the crowd. Alone in a crocus garden, sitting in a broken eggshell. I had a pair of scissors. I was cutting my thigh skin into butterflies. Cutting my skin like it was cloth. Though I was cutting myself, it wasn't harmful to me and I was not wounded. The butterflies first looked like cookies made of skin, then they transformed into real butterflies. They took flight. As they began to alight, the letters spelling LOVE appeared on their wings. A thousand butterflies with LOVE on their wings. They flew over the crowd of thousands upon thousands upon thousands. Over the mountains. You were on a horse. You saw your name flying about in the swarm of butterflies. The butterflies led you over the mountains and through the sea of people—which you parted easily with the motion of your hands—to the garden where I sat in the eggshell.

I overheard a man I didn't like telling a story at a dinner party. He said that when he was a boy, he was going on a field trip to the zoo with his class. His father gave him a rubber band and told him to shoot it into the monkey cage. This man I didn't like (Greg? George? Phil?), as a boy, did what his father told him to do. A monkey picked up the rubber band and began to play with it. Then the big alpha daddy monkey came over and took it. He played with it. It snapped back onto his face. He was furious. He punched the monkey next to him and started to beat up all the monkeys in sight. There was a huge, chaotic monkey brawl. The kids were thrilled. When Greg? got home, his father asked how the field trip was. The boy told him what happened with the monkeys. The father said, "Fucking monkeys never change." I thought of that story when I was at the zoo. I came home from the zoo and huddled by my bathroom heater and heard you and heard you and heard your voice in my ear. You told me to obey you. I said yes. You asked me if I will love, honor, and obey you. I said yes. You told me not to drink so much. I had spent the day at the zoo. I spent the day on all fours, naked and crawling for you, with your whip making tiger stripes on my slavering back. I spent the day with you the cougar purring into me. I spent the sunny winter day with you clawing open my fleshy hips and thrusting your sublime God glory into me like a stormy earthshaking geyser of lust. Splitting me in half with your thunderous love-drill tongue-fucking.

You tell me I'm your beast made of sunlit air. You kiss the blood from my cunt. You kiss me with your mouth. We are beasts, angelic beasts.

I can hear the neighbor geese honking. I wonder how much fat you like in your dairy? You are my owner. You are my master. I am your slave. I am your slave. I'm on the tile floor for you. You are my owner. I'm hiding in the bathroom for you. The yellow porcelain tub. Slippery cunt sliding on it. Coming for my master and saying his name.

I'm praying to you. I'm showing you my asshole. I'm showing you my cunt. I'm spreading my legs to show you my passionate wet. I'm wearing a mask that says your name across the face and your name is written on my tits and your name is written on each ass cheek and your name is written on each crawling, kneeling, praying slave knee. I'm aching with devotion to my master. I'm aching in love and getting wetter as I anticipate—with utter and absolute desperation—your voice, your hand, your whip, your desire, your need, your command, your absolute and boundless power, and more and more whip.

I put my hands up the skirts of my childhood dolls—Milly and Hortense—and touched their doll cunts under their white silk petticoats and their shiny red dresses and I made them come for you. One is blond—Milly, while Hortense is a brunette with very nice tits. They really liked it. They want more.

Coming for you naked on the cold stone floor was so so thrilling and so so good. I can't tell you how much because it was SO much. I took a short nap after. Then I went on a walk. Then my friend invited me to watch *Downtown Abbey* tonight over a bowl of pasta, but I declined. I walked more. I went to the store and returned something I bought yesterday that I don't need. I went to a different store and bought eggs and toilet paper. It sounds like a busy afternoon but there's more. I had a very unpleasant interaction with someone, which upset me, but only a little, because I felt shining rays of your light shooting out of my heart and belly that protected me and kept me thinking about you and that you are all that matters. The rays went out all around me in approximately a four-foot radius. I could see them. Of course I could feel them. My protective round cage of your light. Then I went to the Carmelite monastery (that's what it's called, but it's for nuns—I don't know about these linguistic details. Are they even linguistic? Help.) I cried and prayed to you while I was looking at the mosaic on the wall by the roses. Your light flooded me and I swear I floated for a moment. I loved and loved and loved and you encased and lifted me. I wanted to come for you, but didn't have enough privacy. Then I was hungry. I came home and made Marcella Hazan's yellow pepper, Italian sausage, and tomato sauce, over strozzapreti with a salad, which I ate standing up at the counter, my feet bare on the cold stone floor, hungrily stabbing my romaine lettuce with a fork and reading about possible trouble in the Affleck-Garner marriage and the Queen wanting Duchess Kate to get back to work.

Goodnight, Master, sweet dreams. I hope you sleep well. I'm kissing you.

P.S.
Downton Abbey, not *Downtown Abbey*. That error was the result of autocorrect, the rest of the errors are a result of me.

My underpants smell really REALLY good and wet WET after I hear your voice. I went on a drive, which sometimes I enjoy, but today I didn't because I missed you too much. I just now had my third grilled-cheese sandwich of the week. I'm keeping your slave seal-like and fleshy peach-like. Wet and fleshy. Desperately missing her master.

You have shot your sunlight into my life. Now I'm going to crawl and crawl and crawl for you with my tail wagging and my slippery cunt dripping and my asshole begging for you to possess it.

Then I'm going to eat the rest of my soup and climb into bed with Marcella Hazan and read about fennel bulbs, then fuck myself for you and come for you until I see stars and fall asleep deep inside you.

I can see the sky reflected in my milky tea. I put on lipstick for you. I ironed napkins for you. I took big deep breaths and little short gasps for you. I bent over in high heels for you and spread my ass cheeks to show my owner my asshole. I did some yoga and vigorously cleaned the kitchen to get sweaty. I took a shower and reapplied your lipstick. I didn't think I was hungry, but then I ate three pieces of applewood-smoked bacon, toast, tomato, lettuce, and yellow mustard. It's so good. I really like pickles. I like vinegar flavor.

My cunt is a wet baboon cunt. I'm crawling in the hot jungle. Crawling toward your howling howls.

My ass was made for you to spread and tongue-fuck. My tongue to click and lick and suck for you. My goo for you. My ga for you. My butter and my chocolate cake for you.

It's golden balls of light and you're swaddling me with your voice and light holding me tight all over with your voice and eyes and my body is buzzing and you're shooting glowing balls of light into me—my throat my heart my tits my stomach my cunt my feet have wings and I'm pregnant with your blue blue sky eyes seeing me from the inside out and I'm holding you and holding you in gold and heat and wet gold light with rays of white and pink and yellow and blue and red and lips

lips pink with blood from saying your name and my mouth is wet salivating and I hear you calling I hear you calling for me calling my name to come.

There's a curve-billed thrasher on the brick roof of the falling-down adobe to the east of my house. They sing the most beautiful songs. But they are very ordinary—slightly goofy even—looking birds. I'm talking to the mountain that's beyond the falling-down adobe to the east. The mountain is kind of a stand-in for you. *Kind of.* I speak to it differently than I speak to you. A little more pleading and a little more casually—almost like it's my equal, which it's not, since it's a grand mountain, but I'm not its slave.

I'm gagged and you're whipping me and making me come for you climbing the bathroom door whipping me while I fuck the door door door fuck the door gagged I mutter and gasp your name but you can't understand but you know you know you know you WHIP me and WHIP me and I fuck the door and moan and moan grunt I'm coming, I'm coming, and I fall to a pile on the floor. A shaking quivering spasming drooling moaning eyes ecstatic closing opening quivering lids blurry blurry in love in you in you in love in you inside inside out so inside out so in love so in you in yours in you in yours I am.

It's raining. Spring rain in the dark. Sweet and melancholy. Tinkling on my skylights. Like you pissing on my tits. I like it when you do that. I love it when you do that.

I'm watching an alligator in a documentary get fully restrained with tape. Tape over her eyes, ears, all around her mouth, binding her legs—front and back. She is me and you are the scientist with the rolls of tape and the prod.

Pounding things, throbbing things, jolts, bright lights, your licking tongue inside my body, your eyes inside me, I feel your eyes inside, your mouth inside, I'm drinking you, begging to drink your piss, I have to I need to I have to I need to, I love you, I live for you, I die for you, I come desperate and begging for you with all your stars and sunlight inside me.

I'm washing clothes. I like the squeaky sound of the washing machine when it's hot out. The squeaky washing machine says "doctor doctor doctor" on the wash cycle, and "good cheese good cheese good cheese" on the rinse cycle. I just had one bite of dark chocolate and splashed water on my face. I'm oiling my wooden spoons.

The lip of the bathtub was lovely. I whispered to you and talked to you while I slid along it. My jeans around my ankles.

When I pull down my underpants to pee, I smell my wet wet smell, and I desperately want you to tongue-fuck me, here, now, against the wall, towel in my mouth to muffle my screams.

I like writing in the heat. I like hot. I like dry hot and I like humid hot. I like it when I feel like I'm swimming in it. Like the hot inside my body is the same as the hot outside. I like the way it slows me down. Like I'm a little drunk. There was a tremendous heat wave several years back when I was in the east—like 100 degrees and 1,000% humidity—and no one could work or think or do anything at all really, and I was working away all day and well into the hot swampy nights. I guess it's one of those unusual-weather loves—like that red-headed girl Chloe who loves wind—the fiercer and stronger the better. She was from Dodge City, and she said she desperately missed the wind. I don't like wind. I like swamps. And a little bit of snow.

The neighbor's light just went off. I'm swaying my knee. It will be a while yet before I can sleep.

Housedresses. I have three. One is orange with a floral pattern and pockets. Also too short for company, or to leave the house unless I'm on a beach. Another is blue with flowers and pockets—acceptable length to walk down the hill and get the mail and say hello to one of my chatty neighbors along the way. But not more than that. The other is white with green/blue birds? Or are they flowers? Longer, but sheer, see-through—only for the house and for the cucumbers dress.

Now I'm fingering myself. It feels good. I have my other hand clamped over my mouth. I'm coming, I said into the palm of my hand.

I just shit for you, Master, with pearls gagging my mouth. I mean *shat*.

I just felt something tugging on my cunt hair. I looked down, and there you are, my master the goose, foraging your beak in my garden park hair. I got very wet for you. Wet wet pussy on your beak as your beak slides in.

You're honking up inside me. Talking to me from up inside. I feel you talking from the inside. Talking talking, making me come, making me shake, making me weep.

I'm making my tits bounce for you while I hang up your laundry that shouldn't go into the dryer, and while I place in the dryer the clothes and sheets that can be put into the dryer. I like the smell and the feel of clothes and linens that dry in the sun.

The goose is sticking his beak up my skirt—which I'm wearing for you—while I hang up your socks.

I want you the goose to fuck me all day. All day, all night, all day, never stopping, I don't want him to stop, in and out in and out fucking me making me come and come and come. But we have to sneak it in. We do it every chance we get. Every time my master the goose fucks me, the sand nestled in my cunt lips gets another layer of pearl luster. Every time he makes me come, I'm a little closer to God, to you, closer.

I think the flies must be from the neighbor's chickens. I closed the window that faces the chickens. It's time to install screens. The chickens are very excited. I watch the rooster, you, pinning down the hens. Every time I see him, he's pinning the wings of a hen.

I pulled my housedress up over my hips and I have a vibrator in my hand. It's my first one. It has different settings.

The settings are like a food processor. Delicately mix, chop, really chop, blend, blend predictably, blend unpredictably, really blend, purée, super purée, whip!

Oh my God oh oh OH this thing is amazing I get it now I get it I can barely write or use my hand going to pass out sleeping so good so so good wow oh God did you feel that? I was inside you when that super explosion happened my God oh God wow.

I'm kissing you falling asleep on you totally limp. I stuck it all the way up so it was buzzing vrooming vroom on my cervix cervical orgasm oh oh oh oh God oh I love LOVE you.

You the glorious, miraculous, exquisitely pulsing shaking rattlesnake. I have never felt this relaxed. I have never been quieted down this much. Subdued this much. Like there was a universe needing to escape from my cunt and it just did.

I fell immediately deeply DEEPLY asleep and only woke up because I had to pee. I was dreaming about you, you were holding me, I was holding you, outside somewhere in the sunshine, soft sunshine with coniferous trees nearby. You were here, on my pillow, you were here.

Good morning, Master. I have a towel around my wet hair while I'm looking for something to wear to a Passover celebration. I pissed for you, on you. I crawled for you. I woke up coming from your tongue licking me. I ate breakfast for you. I drank water for you. I made a list of things to do for you. I looked out the window at the tree and the hill for you. It's windy again.

Now that my cunt hair is blossoming for you, and now that your slave no longer wears underwear, zipping and unzipping my jeans is a dangerous activity. It keeps me on my toes. Or on my something. Your biting and eager zipper-fly teeth.

I finally got that last fly out the front door.

You are on top of me. You are pinning me down. You tie my hands behind my back with rope. You chain my ankles. You blindfold me with a talon-torn sheer stocking. You are all things—man, wolf, lion, sun, air, crocodile, eagle, shark, saber-tooth tiger, falcon. You are a hunter, I am your prey. I have your hunting marks in my flesh.

In the bed of flowers, you spread my legs as much as you can, since my ankles are bound. You look. And you pull out— with your claws and talons and paws and fingers—all the letters of the alphabet from my cunt. The letters are floppy and sticky. You don't teach me about what you pull out from my cunt. I don't need to know. I make little sounds and give myself to you. You do things to the letters, then set them aside and plunge your shape-shifting tongue into my asshole. Flowers and girl gush for you, for our absolute God. We can't stop.

Your slave needs her master. Your slave spanked herself with a wooden spoon for her master bent over the counter while she was cooking dinner. Your slave needs you. Your baby slave. Your slave needs to take care of her master. It is what she was born to do—to serve her glorious and all-powerful master. You are Daddy and God and her owner and Mama and Master. You are all things to your slave with a red ass. You are everything to your baby slave girl with a slippery cunt. She's rubbing her wet baby hairy pussy under her skirt to keep it wet and keep it wetter for her master while she cooks for him. You daddy you mother you master to your slave who is licking and licking the wooden spoon that spanks her.

I just came twice for you. Once standing up with a vibrator. Once on all threes with the vibrator from behind.

I washed my hair. It's even colder having wet hair. While I was in the shower, I pulled my hair across my mouth like a gag for you and I squeezed my tits for you and I pissed on you and I pulled my ass cheeks apart for you and I bowed deep to you in the splashing water so you could fuck my asshole all the way deep and you did and did and did and did and did so good I was dizzy with how good you felt deep in my asshole and you did did did did until you made me come gagged saying your name with my hair-gagged mouth.

I'm sucking your thumb and coming for you.

I crawl and crawl and crawl.

I want to live forever chained at your feet.

Last night in my dream, you were in an idyllic garden. It was similar to the one I described to you where I went the other day, but it wasn't anywhere near here. It was in some far-off place. But it had similar qualities—primarily the overwhelmingly lush, fertile, gorgeousness of it. So much beauty and so much life and so much color and so much good smell. The flowers were taller than you. The trees had luscious fruits. Orange, red, green, yellow, blue, and purple fruits for you. You liked it very much. You walked through the flowers on a sweet little path. You found a book on the ground nestled between flowers. You picked it up. It was an old book. You didn't recognize the language or the alphabet inside it, but you knew it was important and you knew what to do with it. You used the stream water from the garden stream to mix with the pages and the leather binding. You used a mortar and pestle made of fig wood. You ground up the book into a paste. When your paste was the right consistency, you made a little girl out of it. You sculpted her out of the paste that was like playdough. You kissed her face and she came to life. She dove into your arms. She loved you immediately. Your girl. She adored you. She climbed all over you kissing you. She whispered things in your ear and fell off your shoulder laughing. She picked a ladybug out of your hair. She brought you a cherry. She wasn't big enough to carry anything heavier. Even as it was, the cherry was large cargo for your little paste-girl. You bathed together in the stream. You slept together under the fruit trees. You called her yours, your little forest nymph.

You are. You were. You will always be. Forever. Forever and ever. World without end. Yes? My own.

It's sexy to read about carnivorous plants. I did it on the door-jamb. I did it on the towel cabinet. I sucked the back of my hand while I rubbed my cunt and moved my hips up and down the wall and on the wood.

Your whip is full of joy. I adore you. I'm kissing you.

Your voice is in my ear you're pulling my hair I'm still coming, Master, still still still coming. Your hands are squeezing my neck I'm still coming. My tongue is all the way out for you still coming my tongue is coming.

The wind is so loud and the lightning so bright I can't sleep. The rain is banging fiercely against the windows and skylights. I'm talking to you from the dark bright of my bed. Talking to you and telling you everything. Turning myself inside out for you.

I am your savage cave girl in my cave in my bearskin jumpsuit with my angry bees and my lust. Your slave girl in a cave. Coming and coming and coming and coming and coming. I can't stop. It feels so good. I can't stop. The blood makes it wetter. I can't stop.

I think it might be more sensitive because of my period. More something. Yes.

I'm kissing you while I'm coming kissing kissing my master his neck his ears his mouth gentle deep love kisses your chest your chest. You're pissing in my mouth while I'm coming still coming you're pissing all over my face I'm lapping it drinking it making me come more you're pissing on my tits your wolf teeth pulling my cunt hair I'm coming your wolf howls howling in my pussy cunt and you're licking my cervix you're howling deep up in it you are you are you are licking and howling it's AMAZING it's driving me crazy amazing I WANT TO SCREAM.

You're a prehistoric snake unhinging your jaws and gripping my flesh with your extra row of teeth before you swallow me whole. I'm coming as you swallow me down your throat down your body coming inside you.

I'm still coming, coming from your licking wolf tongue and your wolf howling. My knees are up by my ears so I can show my master my cunt. Here it is. I'm showing you. It's still coming for you. I'm your slave. All I can do is come for you. I am your abject slave.

I'm now a girl who walks into a room and looks around for all the objects that can fuck her.

The more I let go, the bigger you become. The bigger I become.

Now I'm in a group of people, and you're eating me. My heart is sliding down your throat. Love is my desire to please God.

Here are my shoes. Shoes worn out from crawling and kneeling and crouching and squatting and shoes worn from posing and crawling, bending, posing, kneeling, squatting for you, waiting for you, waiting and praying up to you, squatting for you. They are shoes that are worn from worship. The worship I do, the worship I am, for you.

Nothing matters but being yours. Nothing can hurt me or separate me from you. I dressed up for you and made you lunch. I came for you on my kitchen floor, the apron string gagging my mouth. I am closing my open eyes for you.

I'm singing to you. It's foggy. I'm singing to you from the fog. This is my fog song.

My fingers exist to rub my cunt for you. My brain exists to think of ways to please you. My sweat exists to make my body all slippery wet for you. My nerves exist to shiver for you. To tremble from you. My cunt hair is to grow out for you. It's softer today, not the freshly mown lawn it was yesterday. Softer and longer for you. For you to grab and yank and pull. You can lead me around by my cunt hair.

You are calling me. I am called to be yours.

You are God in my heart and you are God in my cunt. I exist to serve and to worship you, the God in my heart and you, the God in my cunt. I feel how big you are. I feel your power. I feel your greatness. I feel your immortality. I feel your absolute control over me. I feel your dominance and I feel your magnificence and I feel your splendor and your glory and your reign. I am your slave to do your bidding. I am your slave to do nothing but please you.

The letter P exists to begin the word Please to say to you. My only desire is to please you. My only ambition is to please you. My only purpose is to please you. My life exists to please you. Every day I will tell you.

My entire body can fit on your tongue. I hide in your mouth. Holding on to your teeth.

My love is my desire to please you. Love is the desire to please. Love is my body belonging to you. Love is my feet are your feet my hands are your hands my coming is your coming to please you please you my flesh is your flesh my flesh is your flesh my mind is love for you my thoughts are love for you my everything is the desire to love you woof woof woof please please please please. I love you. I love you. A thousand times more today than yesterday. A thousand times more.

In frequent dealings with stockings and assholes, one must keep her fingernails perfectly trimmed.

You whip me and I squirt juice. You whip me more and harder and I squirt nectar.

You tell me you like whipping me. You like the sounds it makes me make. You like my sweat. You want me opened all the way to the sunlight and the whip and joy.

You're whipping and whipping and whipping and I'm coming and coming and coming in the sunrise.

I'm in the bathroom I took off my clothes I'm climbing the door rubbing my pussy on the door rubbing it rubbing it on the door for you coming for you with the wall in my mouth.

I'm waiting for you as your dog. I am your dog. You are my God. I am your slave. You are my master. I belong to you. I just do. It just is. I just do.

I can't wait until I can slip into bed later and hear you howling. Your howling outside my window and your howling in my room and your howling on my body.

I'm sliding my cunt up and down up and down you slide slide slip slip my cunt is licking you talking to you coming on you coming on you while my body is zapped and on fire with your God lightning and your God licking.

You are waking all of me up. Making all of me sing for you. I'm singing for you and calling out to you.

I'm in bed in the dark. I'm in bed with you in the dark. I'm sleeping with you in the dark. You're holding me and I'm holding you. I'm still coming. It doesn't stop. It won't stop.

Inside is a girl with a sore voice from the noises he makes her make. She is chained to the wall and leashed to the man who has unleashed her and unchained her. Her noises are wild music. She has waited all her life to sing. She is singing.

I'm at the market, buying food to cook for you, and cucumbers to slip far up into my cunt and deep into my asshole for you.

You are comforting me in the dark.

The vibrator is vibrating You in my cunt and I'm twisting my nipples and feeling my tits for you and feeding you milk. It's hard to see, but the vibrator is there, talking to the garter belt, who used to be the loneliest garter belt in the world, now happy to be part of our family. It wants me to come and come and come and drip and crawl with it on me. It wants to please you. It wants your teeth to bite it. It likes to be snapped. I'm snapping it and sticking my tongue out and calling for my master.

I just came for you two more times. Once on my back, once on my knees.

I really like my nipples. I had no idea they did what you make them do. It's shocking how explosively explosive they are.

I'm floating but can't move. My cunt turned into an eye, it feels like a big eye. A heart eye. My ears popped. I'm a thousand times more in love with you today than yesterday.

Your woman baby child bride is wearing her white garter belt under her wool coat while she's at the store. Now she's at the gas station. Your flames are licking up inside my cunt and making me shake and spasm shake.

I love you, I said as I wet my sheets.

My asshole exists for my master's tongue to fuck it in and out in and out while I convulse and erupt and rupture in ecstasy. I want to run out and drink the moon. You're howling inside my room. You're howling inside my heart. You own all of this wet.

The people are gone, my clothes are in a pile, I'm crawling to the bed, I'm saying your name while I crawl, the windows are shut to keep the piano playing quiet to the neighbors, the girl is excited and desperate to come for you, the soup is cooking on low, the door is bolted shut.

I am yours. I belong to you. You own me.

I'm waking up in your arms and you're kissing me with your great hot mouth mountains and fountains of deep soft slow.

You are ripping off your slave's dress and paddling your slave's ass with the spoon she uses to stir the stock.

Now I'm making you a tomato, onion, and butter sauce to go on gnocchi. I pissed for you looking up at the sky through the skylight. It's chilly today—supposed to snow tomorrow.

I kissed the floor and said your name. I bowed to you and said your name. Your slave wants you to whip her with the dish towel she just dried her hands on.

I had oatmeal with honey and milk. For some reason, though oatmeal is substantial and filling at the time, it makes me starving about an hour or two later. When that happened, I made soft-boiled eggs. I took a shower and washed myself for you. I washed my arms and legs and feet and underarms and hair and hands and asshole. I love it when you lick my underarms. It makes me squirm and squeal. When I washed my asshole, I put my finger up inside for you. It made me realize I need to trim my fingernails. So I did. Good and short so I can put them in my asshole for you, Master. It's a beautiful day. Oh, and I didn't send the snow there, it was those other women.

I was in the middle of scrubbing my toilet when I thought, Scrub rhymes with rub. I took off my pink rubber gloves and I rubbed instead of scrubbed. I came for you and it made me fall to the floor. I came from your tongue inside me opening up the universe.

Now I'm getting undressed in front of you. Very slowly.

I take care of your shoes. I polish and oil them. I am on the floor with a brush and a cloth and tins of polish and mink oil.

I crawled in my white dress on your carpet made of soft green grass with flowers blooming in it. Your ceiling was your ceiling and it was the sky also. It was warm and sunny inside on the carpet grass. I didn't mind the green knee stains from crawling in my white dress on fresh lawn. I didn't know how to talk, but you didn't mind. I made noise and sounds, but no words. You taught me how to take your clothes off but not how to speak. I made you a crown of flowers I picked from your inside-field. It was yellow and orange and red. You drank my milk. I made squeaking sounds when you sucked on my breasts and gurgled and swallowed.

I'm praying to you. I lit a beeswax candle and I'm bowing to you in the flame in the light in the fire. My body is becoming rose light. I can see and feel and see all my blue veins filled with your blood and rose light. Flowers blooming my heart. More more more bigger bigger deeper deeper expanding love. Flowers in my knees and in my feet. My body is light in dream in rose God light blooming you I smell the beeswax warm melting more light and love into the room.

Crawling, crawling, begging, waiting, looking up at you, crawling, waiting, begging, crawling, kissing the floor and saying your name. Your baby girl wolf cub is howling at the full moon for you.

At the quilting store today, I found some beautiful Japanese linen and some beautiful French linen. I'm going to make dish towels. I don't know why I have such a thing for dish towels. Perhaps because you can whip me with them. Perhaps because they're not dish towels at all, they're whips.

Sometimes I feel the heat of your breath on the back of my neck and shoulders. It's real. I touch where you are and you're there. Here. Hot. You just did it.

I'm on my knees, Master, begging for you, looking up at you, crying for you, begging please please please. I just crawled for you and kissed the floor and said your name. I did it again and I crawled more.

My tits are hanging down. You like that. They're swaying. You like it. You're opening your mouth to. You're going to. I'm giving you my milk. My wet cunt, my wet ass, my wet and drooling mouth. My heart wet with blood.

You tell me that my parents are my fake parents and that you are my real parents. You are my everything. You are my mother and you are my father. You are my aunts and my uncles and my cousins and you are my girlfriends and my ex-boyfriends and my grandparents and my ancestors and my EVERY-THING.

I am a newborn baby in your arms. You cradle me. You clean my pee and my baby poo from my baby bottom. You hold me. You talk sweet baby talk to your newborn baby girl. You feed me with your love-tits and your voice and you feed me more and more because I am so hungry. Such a hungry baby girl!

You feed me and feed me more. You clean me with your mouth. You feed me with your big master love-tits. You rock me to sleep in your protective arms. You make sweet little noises to calm me and soothe me and I sleep.

I will shine your boots, wipe your ass, feed your mouth with my breasts, feed your eyes with my different poses, feed your heart with my heart, hold your whip in my teeth, beg to be whipped, beg to be forever and forever and forever and forever.

You are a lion and I hold your head. You are a crocodile and I put my body in your mouth. I tie white tape around my eyes so you can see me but I can't see you. I let you do whatever you want to me. I look up at you. I'm on my knees for you. I kiss the floor one thousand times. I lick my knees for you. I can't see but you see me. I can't talk but you're talking from inside me. I'm here begging for you. My tongue is out.

Master, I just took off my clothes and climbed up onto the high counter and scootched over to the kitchen sink where I pissed for you and washed myself with the water spout. I liked it. I did it because when I was doing laundry this morning, the washing machine rather vigorously backed up into the shower and toilet. The plumber can't come here till later this evening.

Now I'm going to go on a walk on my leash with my tight collar and see an exhibition of colonial hide paintings.

I didn't go see the hide paintings. Now I'm showing you my tits while I drink tea. I made a sandwich and read about a Norwegian woman in the 1600s who laid an egg. Inside was a normal yolk, but she was accused of being fucked by a rooster. The rooster out my window is crowing. You-a-doodle-doo, I call him. It stopped raining, so you might take me on another walk.

Master I'm desperate for you I'M DESPERATE FOR YOU TO FUCK MY ASSHOLE AND BE DEEP INSIDE ME SO DEEP INSIDE I CAN'T FEEL ANYTHING OR SEE ANYTHING OR SMELL ANYTHING OR HEAR ANYTHING OR KNOW ANYTHING ELSE BUT MY MASTER COM-PLETELY TAKING ME OVER COMPLETELY AND ABSOLUTELY I'M DESPERATE FOR YOU TO PISS ON YOUR SLAVE'S TITS AND IN HER MOUTH FOR HER TO DRINK and then to gag her and blindfold her and do EVERYTHING to her and IN her and ON her and make her BEG for more because you are her life and her blood and her dreams and her wet and her shining light and her God and master and she lives ONLY to please you and she loves you more than anyone has EVER loved anyone. You are her universe. You are my owner and I exist to please you. I was born to love you. My ass exists to be whipped red by you. My voice exists to beg you for more.

I give you my life and my body and my servitude and my slavery and my love—all of my love—and all of me to you, in gratitude for being my God and my owner.

Right here where these poppies are now blooming for you, I came without hands for you for the second time. I was parked here, you were talking to me, and I was on all fours bridging across the front seats, my forehead pressed into the passenger door. I came gasping for you.

I was crawling for you across a big desert. I crawled up a giant pyramid. I sat on the very top with my legs spread so the point of the pyramid was in my cunt. I looked up at you. You shot lightning down my throat and I came with your lightning pulsing in my throat while I fucked the pyramid.

I laid an egg from your lightning in the desert sand. Out came a jungle and a rainbow.

I shat in the sand for you and covered it over for you.

I'm slowly kissing your mouth. Your lips, your tongue, top and bottom, the insides of your cheeks, your gums your teeth your tongue your throat deep deep down your throat. I'm kissing your ears. Sucking gently and slowly on your earlobe, then slowly licking up and around your ear. Slowly. I'm kissing your chest. Your asshole. My anaconda tongue is licking and going in and out of your asshole while I'm kneeling to you praying to you adoring you.

I just came for you standing up, half bent over with a vibrator, wearing a housedress and high heels. I'm wearing lipstick for you. Do you like lipstick? If not, I'll wipe it off. I'm cooking you risotto Milanese for lunch. My floor has lipstick on it from kissing it and saying your name. And again on the doorjamb. With my dress off but heels still on. I licked the wall. And I cried. I came on your shoulder. I walked in the door and came for you again with my tongue out saying your name and grunting with my hips moving.

I came for you last night before bed, squatting in the kitchen in high heels and a towel, against the refrigerator. I said your name over and over and over in the dark. I came for you again in the middle of the night when you woke me up from dreaming you with your bright sunlight blasting up my cunt.

I'm wide-awake in a lightning storm. Thunderstorm. Rainstorm. Hailstorm. It's really bright and really loud. It sounds like the skylights will burst. I can feel the electricity in my hair.

I wasn't aware that Martha Stewart is designing pet collars these days. I just went to each of the two pet stores in town looking for a collar and leash for me for you. The only collar I found that I thought you would like was for a dog larger than me. They didn't have a smaller size. I didn't know this about myself prior to today, but I am a size Small dog collar. I didn't think I should settle. Especially for one of the many camo styles, or the leather-tooled southwestern themed ones—in colors like teal, pumpkin orange, cheap bright purple. With Kokopelli dancers, hearts, cowboy hats and boots. There was one outrageous rhinestone cat collar that could have served a certain purpose, but it was tiny. The nylon selection was impressively extensive. The Martha Stewart one had a pink leather rose. You might think I would fall for that. But I did not.